WE'RE ON YOUR SIDE, CHARLIE BROWN

Selected Cartoons from BUT WE LOVE YOU,
CHARLIE BROWN. Vol. 1

Charles M. Schulz

CORONET BOOKS
Hodder Fawcett Ltd., London

Printed and bound in Great Britain for
Coronet Books,
Hodder Fawcett Ltd,
St. Paul's House, Warwick Lane,
London, EC4P 4AH
by Hazell Watson & Viney Ltd,
Aylesbury, Bucks

ISBN 0 340 10760 X

I'LL BET I WOULD HAVE MADE A GOOD BALD EAGLE!

SCHULZ

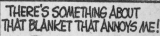

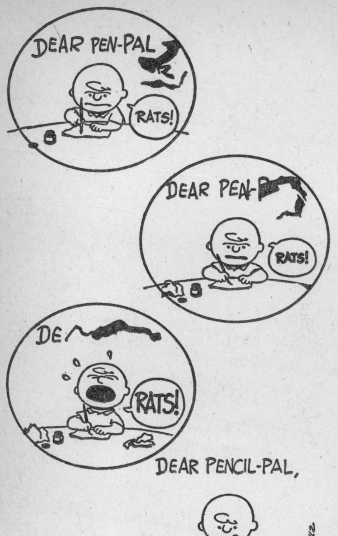

DEAR PENCIL-PAL,

DEAR PENCIL-PAL.

I KNOW YOU ARE REALLY MY PEN-PAL, BUT I AM GOING TO HAVE TO CALL YOU MY PENCIL-PAL.

THIS IS BECAUSE I DO NOT PRINT WELL WITH A PEN.

HOPING YOU WILL NOT BE OFFENDED, I REMAIN YOURS TRULY, CHARLIE BROWN

SCHULZ

LUCY, WHAT'S THE DIFFERENCE BETWEEN A BUG AND AN INSECT?

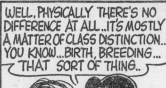

WELL, PHYSICALLY THERE'S NO DIFFERENCE AT ALL...IT'S MOSTLY A MATTER OF CLASS DISTINCTION.. YOU KNOW...BIRTH, BREEDING... THAT SORT OF THING..

I SURE ENVY YOU YOUR KNOWLEDGE OF NATURE..

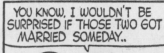

WITH CHARLIE BROWN,
FLYING A KITE IS AN
EMOTIONAL EXPERIENCE

© 1970 United Feature Syndicate, Inc.

Wherever Paperbacks Are Sold

HERE COMES SNOOPY

All these books are available at your bookshop or newsagent, or can be ordered direct from the publisher. Just tick the titles you want and fill in the form below.

....

CORONET BOOKS, P.O. Box 11, Falmouth, Cornwall.

Please send cheque or postal order. No currency, and allow the following for postage and packing:

1 book – 7p per copy, 2–4 books – 5p per copy, 5–8 books – 4p per copy, 9–15 books – 2½p per copy, 16–30 books – 2p per copy in U.K., 7p per copy overseas.

Name...

Address...

....